NUMBERS

BY DORIS ESPINOZA ILLUSTRATED BY TOM HERZ

Harcourt

Orlando   Boston   Dallas   Chicago   San Diego

Visit *The Learning Site!*

www.harcourtschool.com

Numbers are very useful.

People use numbers to count things.

People use numbers to measure things.

People use numbers to compare things.

People use numbers to name things.

People use numbers in music.

Numbers were probably the first things that people wrote.

Early people kept records. They made marks on the walls of caves or on tablets made of clay. This way they could keep track of animals, tools, and time.

Early people also counted on their fingers. It is easy to show the numbers 1 to 10 with fingers. To show larger numbers, people made other signs with their fingers.

When that became too hard, people used beads and boards. It was an easier way to count.

Even today, people use lines called tallies to add numbers. Using tallies is an easy way to count by fives.

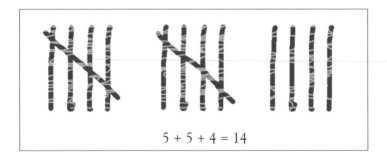

5 + 5 + 4 = 14

Roman Numerals

The Romans used numbers that looked like letters. Some Roman numbers, or numerals, are I, V, and X.

I	=	1
V	=	5
X	=	10

These Roman numerals are added together to make larger numbers.

III	=	3
VIII	=	8
XV	=	15
XX	=	20

Roman numerals are fun to read. They are used on some clocks.

Sometimes you see Roman numerals on the sides of buildings.

Sometimes Roman numerals are used to mark book pages.

Roman numerals sometimes use subtraction. Putting a smaller number in front of a larger number means to subtract it. An *I* in front of a V or X means "one less than."

V = 5	X = 10
IV = 4	IX = 9

Roman numerals can get very long.

Here is a chart of Roman numerals from 1 to 30.

I (1)	II (2)	III (3)	IV (4)	V (5)
VI (6)	VII (7)	VIII (8)	IX (9)	X (10)
XI (11)	XII (12)	XIII (13)	XIV (14)	XV (15)
XVI (16)	XVII (17)	XVIII (18)	XIX (19)	XX (20)
XXI (21)	XXII (22)	XXIII (23)	XXIV (24)	XXV (25)
XXVI (26)	XXVII (27)	XXVIII (28)	XXIX (29)	XXX (30)

There must be an easier way to write numbers!

١٢٣

The number symbols we use today have been around for only about 1,500 years. The Arab people first used them. That's why the numbers we use are called Arabic numerals.

These numbers developed because of trade. People traded things such as spices between Arabia, India, and China. They needed a good way of keeping records. People from different countries had to be able to read the numbers.

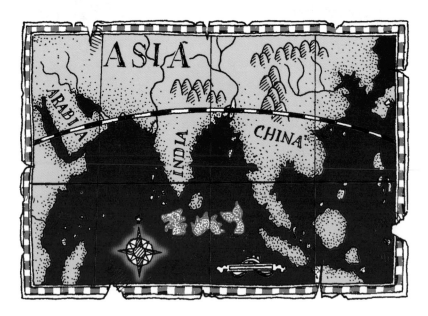

Zero

For a long time, people only counted starting with one. They didn't use zero. There was no symbol for zero.

People probably thought that zero didn't matter. The Roman people didn't write the zero. The Arab people and the Chinese people didn't write the zero either.

But the Indian people did use zero. They invented the symbol for zero. The invention of the zero was the start of the kind of math we use today.

Here are some numbers that use zero.

10 stands for ten.
100 stands for one hundred.
1,000 stands for one thousand.
10,000 stands for ten thousand.
100,000 stands for one hundred thousand.
1,000,000 stands for one million.

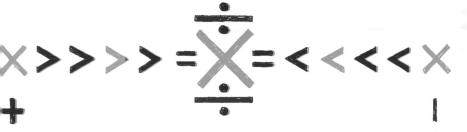

Numbers are symbols. A symbol is something that stands for something else. Ten number symbols are used in math today.

0 1 2 3 4 5 6 7 8 9

These symbols are used to write all the other numbers. For example, the symbol for two is 2. It is used to write the number 12.

Whole Numbers

Whole numbers are every counting number and zero. Zero, 1, 2, 3, 4, 5, and beyond are whole numbers.

A fraction like $\frac{1}{2}$ is not a whole number.

A percent like 40% is not a whole number.

A decimal like 6.7 is not a whole number.

Writing Numbers

Numbers can be written in different ways. Here are two ways numbers can be written.

Number Form	Word Form
1,275	one thousand, two hundred seventy-five

Most math problems are written in number form. Here is a number sentence. It shows addition.

$$15 + 82 = 97$$

Numbers can be written in word form. Here is a subtraction problem. It is written in words.

Question: Ivan was holding five eggs. He dropped three eggs on the floor. How many eggs were left?

Answer: Ivan had two eggs left.

Even and Odd

Some numbers are even, and some are odd. Even numbers can be divided by 2.

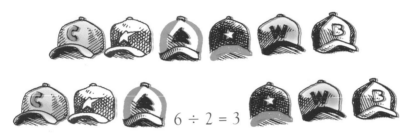

6 ÷ 2 = 3

All even numbers end in 0, 2, 4, 6, or 8. For example, 12, 54, 76, and 98 are even numbers.

Odd numbers cannot be divided by 2. There is always 1 left over. Odd numbers end in 1, 3, 5, 7, or 9.

Prime Numbers

A prime number can be divided only by itself and 1.

3 ÷ 3 = 1	17 ÷ 17 = 1
3 ÷ 1 = 3	17 ÷ 1 = 17

Here are all the prime numbers from 1 to 100. The number 2 is the only even prime number.

2	3	5	7	11
13	17	19	23	29
31	37	41	43	47
53	59	61	67	71
73	79	83	89	97

You can count to 10 in other languages!
Every Language Counts!

Number	Spanish	German	English
1	uno	eins	one
2	dos	zwei	two
3	tres	drei	three
4	cuatro	vier	four
5	cinco	fünf	five
6	seis	sechs	six
7	siete	sieben	seven
8	ocho	acht	eight
9	nueve	neun	nine
10	diez	zehn	ten